Zoo Animals

MONKEYS
AT THE ZOO

By Seth Lynch

Gareth Stevens
PUBLISHING

Please visit our website, www.garethstevens.com. For a free color catalog of all our high-quality books, call toll free 1-800-542-2595 or fax 1-877-542-2596.

Library of Congress Cataloging-in-Publication Data

Names: Lynch, Seth, author.
Title: Monkeys at the zoo / Seth Lynch.
Description: New York : Gareth Stevens Publishing, [2020] | Series: Zoo animals | Includes index.
Identifiers: LCCN 2018039584| ISBN 9781538239346 (paperback) | ISBN 9781538239360 (library bound) | ISBN 9781538239353 (6 pack)
Subjects: LCSH: Monkeys–Juvenile literature. | Zoo animals–Juvenile literature.
Classification: LCC QL737.P9 L95 2020 | DDC 599.8–dc23
LC record available at https://lccn.loc.gov/2018039584

First Edition

Published in 2020 by
Gareth Stevens Publishing
111 East 14th Street, Suite 349
New York, NY 10003

Copyright © 2020 Gareth Stevens Publishing

Editor: Therese Shea
Designer: Katelyn E. Reynolds

Photo credits: Cover, p. 1 vblinov/Shutterstock.com; p. 5 FamVeld/Shutterstock.com; p. 7 Don Mammoser/Shutterstock.com; pp. 9, 24 (tail) ChameleonsEye/Shutterstock.com; p. 11 Julia Moiseenko/Shutterstock.com; p. 13 Iakov Filimonov/Shutterstock.com; p. 15 Henk Bogaard/Shutterstock.com; pp. 17, 24 (mandrill) SawBear/Shutterstock.com; pp. 19, 24 (troop) Nick Fox/Shutterstock.com; p. 21 Ryan M. Bolton/Shutterstock.com; p. 23 Evikka/Shutterstock.com.

Printed in the United States of America

CPSIA compliance information: Batch #CS19GS: For further information contact Gareth Stevens, New York, New York at 1-800-542-2595.

Contents

I see monkeys
at the zoo.
I learn a lot!

Most monkeys
live in trees.

Monkeys have tails.

Some tails are small.

11

There are more than 200 kinds of monkeys!

13

Baboons are monkeys.
They live on the ground.

The largest monkey
is the mandrill.

A group of monkeys
is a troop.

Monkeys are smart.
Monkeys are funny!

21

I like the monkeys
at the zoo!

Words to Know

mandrill

tail

troop

Index